Ladybird

Spelling and Grammar

compiled by
DOROTHY PAULL
designed and illustrated by
JOHN BRADFORD
of Hurlston Design

The alphabet

The word *alphabet* is formed from two words, *alpha* and *beta*, which are the first two letters of the Greek alphabet.

The English language has developed very gradually from several more ancient languages. Our present day alphabet of twenty six letters forms the basis of the language.

Two sentences often used to train typists contain all twenty six letters:

Whenever the black fox jumped, the squirrel gazed very suspiciously.
The quick brown fox jumps over the lazy dog.

The alphabet consists of five *vowels* – **a e i o u** –
and twenty one *consonants* **b c d f g h j k l m n p q r s t v w x y z.**
The word *vowel* comes from the Latin word
vocalis meaning *voice.*
Consonant comes from the Latin word
consonare meaning *to sound together.*

Most words contain some vowels and there are a few which contain all five vowels:

facetious   abstemious   tambourine

A few words do not have any vowels at all but they usually have the letter **y** instead, which is used as a vowel.

hymn   why   lynch

CAPITALS or UPPER CASE LETTERS

ABCDEFGHIJKLMNOPQRSTUVWXYZ

LOWER CASE LETTERS

abcdefghijklmnopqrstuvwxyz

The upper and lower cases were the cases in which printers kept their metal type.

The arrangement of the letters is based on frequency of use. The most-used letter is **e**.

4

Contents

Acknowledgment:
The compiler and publishers would like to thank
Andrew M Hunt BA (Hons) Dip Ed for his help during the
preparation of this book.

Ladybird books are widely available, but in case of
difficulty may be ordered by post or telephone from:

Ladybird Books – Cash Sales Department
Littlegate Road Paignton Devon TQ3 3BE
Telephone 0803 554761

A catalogue record for this book is available
from the British Library

Published by Ladybird Books Ltd Loughborough Leicestershire UK
Ladybird Books Inc Auburn Maine 04210 USA

EFTA European Free Trade Association

EHF extremely high frequency

ENT ear, nose and throat

ERM Exchange Rate Mechanism

ESN educationally sub-normal

ESP extra-sensory perception

ETA estimated time of arrival

ETD estimated time of departure

FA Football Association

FBI Federal Bureau of Investigation (USA)

FC Football Club

FO Foreign Office

Fr. Father; Friar; France

GB Great Britain

GBH grievous bodily harm

GCSE General Certificate of Secondary Education

GDR German Democratic Republic

GMT Greenwich Mean Time

GP general practitioner (doctor)

HB hard black (pencil lead)

HGV heavy goods vehicle

HM His/Her Majesty; Headmaster; Headmistress

HMI His/Her Majesty's Inspector

HMS His/Her Majesty's Service or Ship

HMSO His/Her Majesty's Stationery Office

HRH His/Her Royal Highness

IBA Independent Broadcasting Authority

ICI Imperial Chemical Industries

IMF International Monetary Fund

IOU I owe you (written promise to pay)

IQ intelligence quotient

IRA Irish Republican Army

ITA Independent Television Authority (now IBA)

JP Justice of the Peace

Jr. junior

K2 2nd highest mountain in world, in Kashmir – 8610m

KGB Komitet Gosudarstvennoi Bezopasnosti – Russian secret police

LEA Local Education Authority

LP long playing record; Lord Provost; low pressure

MA Master of Arts

MBE Member of the Order of the British Empire

MC Master of Ceremonies

MD Managing Director; Medical Dept; Doctor of Medicine

MI Military Intelligence

MI5 Military Intelligence section 5

MI6 Military Intelligence section 6

MOD Ministry of Defence

MOT Ministry of Transport

NAAFI Navy, Army & Air Force Institutes

NALGO National Association of Local Government Officers

NASA National Aeronautics and Space Administration (USA)

NATO North Atlantic Treaty Organisation

NB *nota bene* – Latin for note well

NCB National Coal Board

NCCL National Council for Civil Liberties

NCO non-commissioned officer

NEC National Exhibition Centre

NF National Front

NFU National Farmers' Union

Abbreviations continued on inside back cover

The alphabet we use is the Roman alphabet.
It developed over thousands of years through Egyptian hieroglyphs, and Phoenician and Greek alphabets.

Egyptian	Phoenician	Greek	Roman

Uses for the alphabet

Reference books, directories, dictionaries and filing systems all use the alphabet as a means of ordering information.

In the UK letters are used together with numbers on car registration plates. These plates give specific information.

This number and the letter U show the number of plates issued so far in year A

the year in which registered from August 1st (83-84)

the town or city in which registered

Before August 1983 when the new sequence was introduced, a similar system was used but the year letter was at the end eg ASD 498 Y.

The USA has no national system. Each state has its own method of registration.

In the UK postcodes also contain letters and numbers. Using the postcode, the Post Office sorting office can sort letters very quickly by machine.

small section of area

main city or town in postal area

CV 13 OLZ

the street or part of a street

In the USA, ZIP codes use numbers only to indicate the town or city, eg 80302 is the ZIP code for Boulder, Colorado.

Sentences

A sentence consists of a group of words, one of which must be a VERB. The verb is the action or doing word. The person or thing doing the action is the *subject* of the sentence. The subject is either a NOUN or a PRONOUN:

*The **boy** bounced the ball.*

If the action is being done to someone or something, that someone or something is the *object* of the sentence, and is also a noun or a pronoun:

*The boy bounced the **ball**.*

Other groups of words also do specific jobs in a sentence. A word telling you more about the boy or the ball is an ADJECTIVE:

*The **big** boy bounced a **blue** ball.*

When we introduce a word to tell us more about how he bounced the ball, we use an ADVERB:

*The big boy **lazily***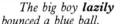
bounced a blue ball.

The words *the* and *a* are ARTICLES: *the* is a particular or **definite article** and *a* (or *an*) is any article or the **indefinite article**. They have no meaning themselves but refer directly to the noun which follows them.

*Give me **a** book from **the** shelf.*

An is used before a word that starts with a vowel, eg *an egg*. Some words starting with **h** also require *an* before them – *an heir, an hour*. (The **h** remains silent.)

A sentence always starts with a capital letter and ends with a full stop (.), a question mark (?) or an exclamation mark (!).

If we make the sentences longer by adding a phrase (a group of words), or a sentence, we need a CONJUNCTION:

*The big boy lazily bounced a blue ball **and** it rolled away from him.*

and is the conjunction which joins the two parts of this sentence together.

it is used instead of *the ball* and is a pronoun.

him is used instead of *the boy* and is also a pronoun.

} Pronouns can be used to replace nouns.

away tells us more about the way the ball rolled, and is an adverb.

from is a PREPOSITION which is used before a noun or pronoun.

Words such as ***Ah! Oh! Eh!*** are INTERJECTIONS. These are sometimes used to express an emotion.

NONSENSE SENTENCES

A sentence can contain a subject, verb and object but be nonsense. This sentence uses subject, verb, object and adverbs, adjectives, conjunctions, etc:

Green elephants knit beautifully if they eat garden gates.

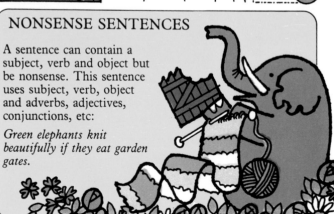

Nouns

A noun is a word which refers to a person, a place, a thing or a title. **Common nouns** do not have capital letters (unless they begin a sentence). **Proper nouns** refer to one particular object, place or person and always start with a capital letter.

Common Nouns

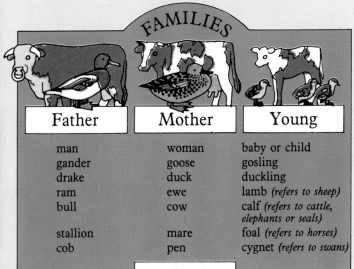

FAMILIES

Father	Mother	Young
man	woman	baby or child
gander	goose	gosling
drake	duck	duckling
ram	ewe	lamb *(refers to sheep)*
bull	cow	calf *(refers to cattle, elephants or seals)*
stallion	mare	foal *(refers to horses)*
cob	pen	cygnet *(refers to swans)*

Diminutives

A diminutive is a small version of something larger.

booklet is from *book*
rivulet is from *river*
piglet is from *pig*

Some nouns indicate size.

a speck
a splinter

Abstract nouns

These nouns name a quality, state or action, rather than a thing.

honesty
corruption
love
hope

Concrete nouns

These nouns are the names of things which can be seen, touched, tasted or smelt.

torch
car
book
apple

Homes

Some nouns indicate the home of a specific type of person or animal.

Person	Home
monk	monastery
minister	manse
king/queen	palace
parson	parsonage
farmer	farm
vicar	vicarage

Creatures	Home		
badger	sett	birds	nest *or* aviary
fox	earth	bees	hive *or* apiary
hare	form	dog	kennel
otter	holt	cow	byre *or* shed
squirrel	drey	rabbit	warren

Nouns continued

Gender denotes sex: masculine, feminine or neuter

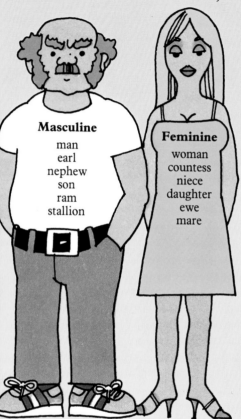

Masculine
man
earl
nephew
son
ram
stallion

Feminine
woman
countess
niece
daughter
ewe
mare

Common gender
(can be either)

person
baby
friend
owner
pupil
teacher
visitor

Neuter gender
(neither male nor female)

apple   envelope   kettle
chimney   garage   umbrella

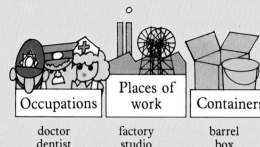

Occupations	Places of work	Containers	Sounds
doctor	factory	barrel	shriek
dentist	studio	box	buzz
florist	garage	cruet	croak
mechanic	office	envelope	squeal
teacher	hospital	tin	groan

THE FIVE SENSES
used to perceive the world.

hearing
sight
smell
taste
touch

THE FOUR ELEMENTS
thought by the ancient world
to make up the universe.

air
fire
earth
water

Collective nouns

Collective nouns are singular words which indicate a group or collection of individuals.

   eg *A **swarm** of bees* is *in the apple tree.*

When the collective noun refers to something specific, it has capital letters.

   eg *the British Government, Parliament*

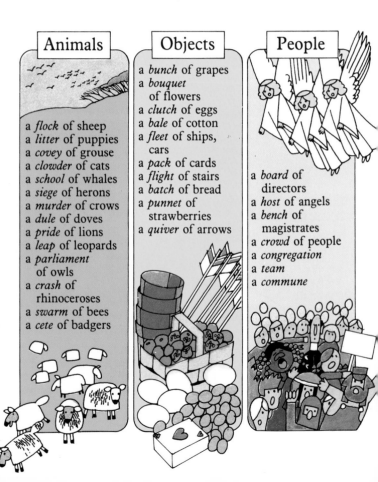

Animals

a *flock* of sheep
a *litter* of puppies
a *covey* of grouse
a *clowder* of cats
a *school* of whales
a *siege* of herons
a *murder* of crows
a *dule* of doves
a *pride* of lions
a *leap* of leopards
a *parliament* of owls
a *crash* of rhinoceroses
a *swarm* of bees
a *cete* of badgers

Objects

a *bunch* of grapes
a *bouquet* of flowers
a *clutch* of eggs
a *bale* of cotton
a *fleet* of ships, cars
a *pack* of cards
a *flight* of stairs
a *batch* of bread
a *punnet* of strawberries
a *quiver* of arrows

People

a *board* of directors
a *host* of angels
a *bench* of magistrates
a *crowd* of people
a *congregation*
a *team*
a *commune*

Proper nouns

These always have a capital letter and refer to a specific
person, place or thing.

Places

Australia	London
Barnsley	South America
Denmark	Paris
Europe	New York

People

(real or fictitious)
Red Riding Hood
Sherlock Holmes
John Paul II
Daley Thompson
Julius Caesar
Gandhi

Titles

Star Wars

Paddington Bear

Hamlet

The Ascent of Man

13

Pronouns

A pronoun is used in place of a noun to avoid repetition. There are three main groups:

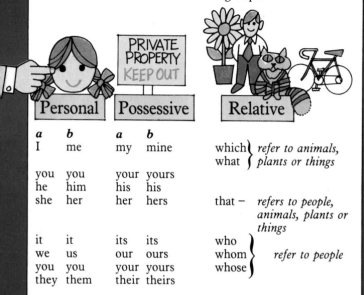

Personal		Possessive		Relative

a	*b*	*a*	*b*	
I	me	my	mine	which / what — *refer to animals, plants or things*
you	you	your	yours	
he	him	his	his	
she	her	her	hers	that — *refers to people, animals, plants or things*
it	it	its	its	who
we	us	our	ours	whom — *refer to people*
you	you	your	yours	whose
they	them	their	theirs	

When the noun is doing the action – ie when it is the subject of the sentence – use a pronoun from column *a*:
personal – ***You** and **I** will go together.*
possessive – column *a* plus the noun: ***Her** hair is very curly.*

When the noun is being acted upon – ie when it is the object of the sentence – use a pronoun from column *b*:
personal – *The teacher shouted at **him** and **me**.*
possessive – *The book is **hers**.*

After a preposition (eg *from, after*), always treat the pronoun as the object of the sentence and use a word from column *b*:
*The dog chased after **him**.*

Relative pronouns refer back to an earlier noun or pronoun:
*Susan gave me a book **which** I had not read.*

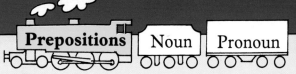

Prepositions | Noun | Pronoun

A preposition is used before a noun or pronoun to indicate its **place** (eg *above, behind*), **position** (eg *on, among*) or **time** (eg *since, until*).

Some other prepositions:

onto	in	across	against	at
through	over	below	between	with
by	within	beyond	after	beneath
upon	beside	off	into	under(neath)
around	along	towards	up	over(head)

*The frog jumped **into** the pond and disappeared **beneath** the surface.*

Con junctions

Conjunctions join together two words, two phrases or two parts of a sentence: eg *You **and** I are going into town today.*
*We can't stay **because** it is late.*

and	but	because	that	or
if	before	since	yet	as
although	for	while	unless	both
either/or	neither/nor	wherever	until	till
lest	even if	except that	so that	

15

Adjectives   Noun

An adjective is used to tell more about a noun or pronoun.
It is often referred to as a describing word. An adjective
usually comes immediately before a noun in a sentence.
More than one adjective can be used with each noun or
pronoun. When describing a pronoun, the adjective follows
the verb.

eg *After falling in the **muddy** water, they were **wet**.*

Adjectives fall into three groups:

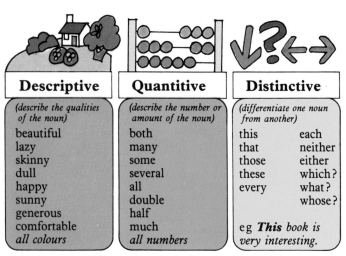

Descriptive	**Quantitive**	**Distinctive**
(describe the qualities of the noun)	*(describe the number or amount of the noun)*	*(differentiate one noun from another)*
beautiful	both	this each
lazy	many	that neither
skinny	some	those either
dull	several	these which?
happy	all	every what?
sunny	double	whose?
generous	half	
comfortable	much	
all colours	*all numbers*	eg ***This** book is very interesting.*

Descriptive adjectives are often formed from a noun:
sunny from *sun*
Others relating to animals are often formed from Latin
words for that animal:
feline from *felis* for cat
bovine from *bovis* for bull
canine from *canis* for dog
leonine from *leo* for lion

The opposite page shows the *positive* forms of adjectives. These are used when only one thing is being described.

When an adjective is used to compare two or more things, it changes form.

*The **tall** girl came into the room.* (one girl: use the *positive* form)	*This girl is **taller** than that one.* (two girls: use the *comparative* form)	*That girl is the **tallest** in the room.* (more than two girls: use the *superlative* form)

Positive	Comparative	Superlative
high	higher	highest
dull	duller	dullest
Exceptions:		
good	better	best
bad	worse	worst

When an adjective has two or more syllables, *more* and *most* are used to form the comparative and superlative.

handsome	*more* handsome	*most* handsome
beautiful	*more* beautiful	*most* beautiful
unusual	*more* unusual	*most* unusual

*The **most beautiful** butterfly I have ever seen came into the garden today.*

17

Verbs

A verb is the most important word in a sentence; it is the action or *doing* word. Without it we are unable to make a sentence.

Examples:

You read this page. and *Read this.* are both sentences.

You this page is not a sentence.

Read is the word which makes the difference. It is the verb.

The person doing the action is the *subject* of the sentence. Sometimes the subject is doing something to someone or something. That is the *object* of the sentence.

Transitive verbs pass an action over from the subject to the object. **Intransitive verbs** do not pass an action.

Transitive

need an object

to give	to find
to do	to catch
to make	to ask

eg *The boy catches a fish.*

Intransitive

do not need an object

to speak	to lie
to listen	to seem
to sit	to die

eg *The teacher speaks.*

✓ Need an object

✗ Do not need an object

Verbs: tenses

The form of the verb which indicates when the action takes place is called its **tense**, from the Latin word *tempus* meaning time.

Present tense

(action is happening now)
I help
you help
she/he helps
we help
you help (plural)
they help

Past tense

(action has happened)
I helped
you helped
she/he helped
we helped
you helped (plural)
they helped

Future tense

(action will happen)
I shall help
you will help
she/he will help
we shall help
you will help (plural)
they will help

Conditional tense

(action may happen if...)
I should help
you would help
she/he would help
we should help
you would help (plural)
they would help

Participles: past and present

Participles are used with another verb in a sentence to change the tense. The other verbs, called auxiliary (helping) verbs, are often forms of the verbs *to be* or *to have* (is, are, am, was, were, have, had).

burnt – past participle
Joan of Arc was **burnt** at the stake.

burning – present participle
The fire is **burning** brightly.

Participles are also used as adjectives, to describe nouns, etc.

*The **burnt** toast was inedible. John warmed his hands by the brightly **burning** fire.*

burnt and **burning** are used here as adjectives.

Present participles	Past participles
(always end in -ing)	*(usually end in -en, -ed or -t)*
speaking	spoken
doing	done
playing	played
crying	cried
forgetting	forgotten
catching	caught

Auxiliary verbs – tenses

Sometimes an auxiliary verb is used with a participle in the present and past tenses.

*I **am** helping*

*I **was** helped*
*I **had** helped*

Present tense
I *drive* to work every day.
I *am driving* today.

Past tense
I *forgot* to take a coat.
I *have forgotten* to buy some bread.

Forms of *should* and *would* are used as auxiliary verbs to form the future and conditional tenses.

Future tense
You *will get* your birthday cards in the morning.

Conditional tense
The school team *should reach* the final if it wins this round.
I *would expect* you to behave yourself in school.

can and may

Can I do something? means, 'Am I physically able to do something?'
eg *Can I play football with a sore foot?*

May I do something? means, 'Will I be allowed to do it by someone else?'
eg *May I play football with you, please?*

Adverbs

The word adverb means *added word*. An adverb tells more about a verb, an adjective or another adverb. It is usually placed immediately before or after the word it is describing. There are three basic groups which tell **how**, **when** or **where** something happens.

How		When	Where
easily	softly	soon	here
quickly	heavily	often	there
noisily	eagerly	yesterday	everywhere
These are formed by		always	somewhere
adding **ly** *to the*		after	along
adjective		seldom	beside

Other adverbs tell how many times or how much something is done, e g *twice*.

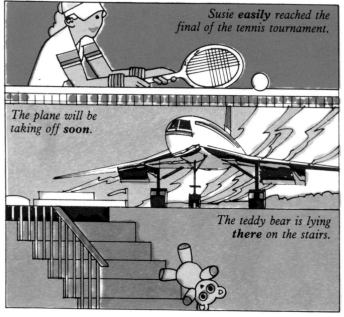

Susie **easily** reached the final of the tennis tournament.

The plane will be taking off **soon**.

The teddy bear is lying **there** on the stairs.

Adverbs, like adjectives, also have comparative and superlative forms. These are formed by using **more** and **most** or **less** and **least** with an adverb.

*The thrush moved **more quickly** than the snail.*

*The robin is one of the **most easily** recognised birds.*

*Foxes hunt for food **less often** in daytime.*

Note: Many prepositions, adjectives and adverbs are the same words. Their positions and functions in a sentence determine what they are called.
eg *My only teacher said so.* **Only** is an adjective.
Only my teacher said so. Here **only** is an adverb.

Singular and plural

Singular refers to *just one thing*.
Plural refers to *more than one thing*.

- Some nouns require only an *s* to form the plural:
  cat/*cats* balloon/*balloons* dog/*dogs*

- For ease of pronunciation, some nouns require *es* to form the plural:
  dish/*dishes* potato/*potatoes* fox/*foxes* dress/*dresses*

- A few nouns ending in *o* require only an *s*:
  photo/*photos* avocado/*avocados* solo/*solos*

- Those nouns ending in *y* following a consonant change *y* to *i* and add *es*:
  party/*parties* lady/*ladies* fly/*flies* city/*cities*
  Exceptions: lay-by/*lay-bys* trilby/*trilbys* all names

  - Nouns ending in *y* following a vowel only add *s*:
    day/*days* monkey/*monkeys* valley/*valleys* boy/*boys*

  - Most nouns ending in *f* or *fe* add *s*:
    chief/*chiefs* roof/*roofs* giraffe/*giraffes*

  - However, some nouns ending in *f* or *fe* change the *f* or *fe* to *v* and add *es*:
    sheaf/*sheaves* wife/*wives* calf/*calves*

  - Nouns ending in *um* change *um* to *a*:
    bacterium/*bacteria* medium/*media*

  - A few nouns have plurals which do not fit into any of the above groups:
    goose/*geese* child/*children* oasis/*oases* foot/*feet* tooth/*teeth* mouse/*mice*

  - Some words keep the same form in the plural:
    salmon deer aircraft sheep trout

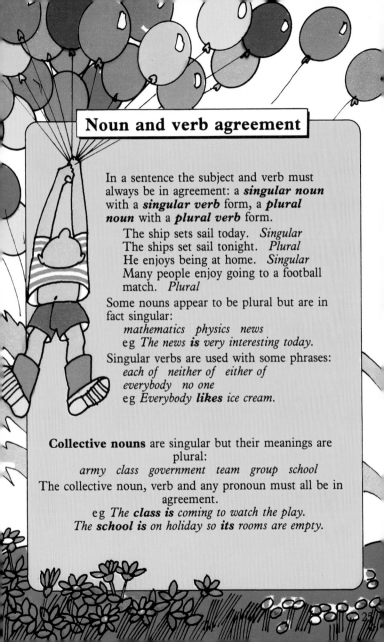

Noun and verb agreement

In a sentence the subject and verb must always be in agreement: a *singular noun* with a *singular verb* form, a *plural noun* with a *plural verb* form.

> The ship sets sail today. *Singular*
> The ships set sail tonight. *Plural*
> He enjoys being at home. *Singular*
> Many people enjoy going to a football match. *Plural*

Some nouns appear to be plural but are in fact singular:

> *mathematics   physics   news*
> eg *The news **is** very interesting today.*

Singular verbs are used with some phrases:

> *each of   neither of   either of*
> *everybody   no one*
> eg *Everybody **likes** ice cream.*

Collective nouns are singular but their meanings are plural:

> *army   class   government   team   group   school*

The collective noun, verb and any pronoun must all be in agreement.

> eg *The **class** **is** coming to watch the play.*
> *The **school** **is** on holiday so **its** rooms are empty.*

Apostrophes

The apostrophe (') is used for two very different purposes:

1 *to show something belongs to someone*

Singular	Plural
*a **boy's** shoes*	*the **boys'** shoes*
*an old **man's** beard*	*the old **men's** beards*
*the **dog's** dinner*	*the **dogs'** dinner*

the dog's dinner

the dogs' dinner

THE APOSTROPHE COMES BEFORE THE **S** IN THE SINGULAR.
Exceptions: its ours yours theirs hers his eg *The cat opened **its** mouth.*

THE PLURAL HAS THE APOSTROPHE AFTER THE PLURAL FORM. ADD AN **S** WHERE THE PLURAL DOES NOT HAVE ONE.
eg *men **men's***

2 *to show that a letter or letters are missing from a word*

eg *I **can't** decide where to go.*
   ***There's** no school tomorrow.*

I have...*I've*   who have...*who've*   it is...*it's*
you will...*you'll*   you have...*you've*   cannot...*can't*
does not...*doesn't*   do not...*don't*   will not...*won't*
shall not...*shan't*   have not...*haven't*
all is well...*all's well*   of the clock...*o'clock*
there is...*there's*   is not...*isn't*   who would...*who'd*

Types of sentences

Simple sentences

A simple sentence conveys
one idea or thought and has
one verb:

> *Julian **has** a rabbit.*
> *Sarah and James **ride** their bicycles.*

Complex sentences

A complex sentence conveys more than one idea or thought
and has more than one verb:

> *Julian **has** a rabbit that **lives** in a hutch.*

Complex sentences can be made into simple sentences:

> *Rachel found a brooch which was very valuable.*

can become:

> *Rachel found a very valuable brooch.*

Compound sentences

Two or more simple sentences can be put together using
conjunctions to form compound sentences:

> *On nice days Sarah and James ride their bicycles.*
> *They do not go out if it rains.*

can become:

> *On nice days, Sarah and James ride their bicycles, **but** they
> do not go out if it rains.*

Some important

In English there are many spelling irregularities and exceptions. Here are some helpful spelling guidelines:

Silent *e*

When a word ends in a silent *e* the earlier vowel says its *name* instead of its *sound*:

In *cape* the *a* is long…(compare this with *cap*)

eg *code* *bite* *cute*

Adding an ending

- When adding *ing, er, able, ious, en, ous, y, age* or *ish* to words ending in *e*, leave off the *e*:

  take/*taking* fame/*famous* bone/*bony* believe/*believable*

  Exceptions: mile/*mileage* singe/*singeing*
  agree/*agreeable – agreeing*

  Keep the e when adding endings beginning with a consonant: *ment* *worthy* *less* *ful*
  tasteless *advancement* *hopeful* *praiseworthy*

- When adding *full* to a word, drop the final *l*:

  beauty/*beautiful* care/*careful*

- For words ending in *ge*, keep the *e* when adding *able* or *ous*:

  manage/*manageable*

- When adding *ing* to words (mainly verbs) ending in *ie*, *e* is dropped and *i* becomes *y*:

  die/*dying* lie/*lying*

- For words ending in *y* following a consonant, change *y* to *i* before adding *es, er, eth, ly, ness* or *ed*:

  forty/*fortieth* busy/*busily, business*
  occupy/*occupied* early/*earlier* apology/*apologies*

- Words ending in *y* following a vowel, keep the *y* when adding the endings *er, ing* or *ed*:

  pray/*praying, prayer, prayed*
  fray/*fraying, frayed*
  say/*saying*

spelling rules

ie and ei

- When *ie* and *ei* sound like *ee* as in *cheese* (eg *yield*), then *i* comes before *e* *except after* *c*:

  believe frieze receive retrieve conceit cashier

  Exceptions: *weird seize weir species*

- Sometimes *ei* says *i*:

  height neither eiderdown either sleight

- *ei* and *ie* can sound like *e* as in *egg*:

  friend leisure

- or like *ai* as in *rain*: *neighbour skein reign eight*

- or like *i* as in *give*: *sieve*

Doubling final consonants

- When a word of one syllable ends in a single consonant, following a single vowel, double the consonant before adding *ed, er, est* or *ing*:

  wag/*wagged* bat/*batter* big/*biggest* run/*running*

  Words ending in *r, x, w* or *y* are exceptions to this rule.

  box/*boxer* saw/*sawing*

- When another consonant or a pair of vowels comes before the final consonant, simply add the ending:

  belt/*belted* bail/*bailing* tall/*taller* great/*greatest*

- When a word ends in *l* following a vowel, double the *l* before adding *er, ed* or *ing*:

  travel/*traveller* cancel/*cancelled* signal/*signalling*

  Exception: parallel/*paralleled*

Silent letters

We don't always
pronounce every letter in
a word. Silent letters can
occur at the beginning, middle or end of a word.

b *plumb lamb tomb doubt*

c *scythe scissors*

ch *yacht*

d *bridge wedge hedge*

g *sign* (but not in *signal*)
gnash gnat gnaw

gh *bright high bough*
through eight

h *heir hour*

k *knock know knight*

l *talk yolk folk*

m *mnemonics*

n *hymn autumn column*

p *pneumonia psalm receipt*

s *island*

t *listen glisten whistle*

u *biscuit guard*

w *write wrist wreck*

ph *pronounced f*

photograph telegraph telephone elephant physical orphan

gh *pronounced f*

cough trough rough laugh draught

gh *pronounced g*

ghost ghastly gherkin ghetto ghoul aghast

Words with a *q*

In the English language, *q* is almost always followed by *u*:
    queue quick conquer plaque
(Some proper nouns, for example place names, may disobey this rule e g *Qatar*.)

DO NOT CONFUSE SOME RELATED NOUNS AND VERBS:

noun	verb
advice	to advise
practice	to practise
licence	to license

e g *The man was grateful for the good* **advice**.   NOUN
She **practised** *the song every day.*   VERB
The noun is always spelled with **c**.
The verb is always spelled with **s**.

30

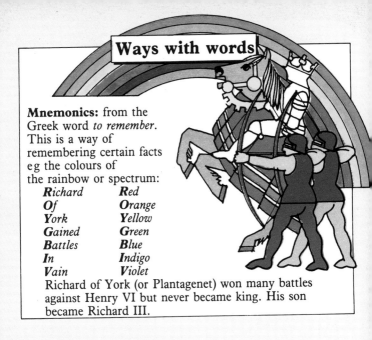

Ways with words

Mnemonics: from the Greek word *to remember*. This is a way of remembering certain facts e g the colours of the rainbow or spectrum:

Richard	*Red*
Of	*Orange*
York	*Yellow*
Gained	*Green*
Battles	*Blue*
In	*Indigo*
Vain	*Violet*

Richard of York (or Plantagenet) won many battles against Henry VI but never became king. His son became Richard III.

Palindrome: a word, phrase or sentence which reads the same backwards as forwards:

level   madam   deed
Was it a cat I saw?
Able was I ere I saw Elba. (This relates to Napoleon's exile on the island of Elba.)

Some dates are also the same in reverse as forwards:
28.7.82   19.2.91

Anagram: an anagram is the re-arrangement of all the letters in a word to make a new word. It is frequently used in crossword puzzles:

e g *angered* is an anagram of *enraged*

Acronyms: an acronym is a word formed from the initial letters of other words:

OPEC   AWOL   NAAFI   NATO   NALGO
See endpapers for definitions.

Prefixes and suffixes

The meaning of a word can be changed by adding groups of letters to it. **Prefixes** (from the Latin *pre*, before) are groups of letters added before a word; **suffixes** (from the Latin *suff*, after) are added after a word.

PREFIXES			MEANINGS	EXAMPLES
a			on as in	afloat aboard
a	*ab*	*abs*	from away	absent averse
ad	*ac*	*ar*	to	advise accept arrival
ante			before	ante meridiem *(am before noon or morning)*
bi	*bis*		two or twice	biennial bicycle biscuit *(cooked twice)*
circum			around	circumspect circumference
com			with together	companion communicate
contra			against	contradict contrary
de			down	detract deter demote
dis	*dif*		not	distaste differ
ex			out of	exit exhale expire
fore			before	foreword forecast

PREFIXES		MEANINGS	EXAMPLES
im	*in*	into	import include
in	*im*	not	incapable impossible
inter		between	interval interrupt
mis		wrong	mistake misapply
ob		against	obstruct object
post		after	postpone postwar
pre		before	prefix preface prepare
pro		for forth	propose profit produce
re		back again	repeat remain retake
sub		under below	substandard submarine
trans		across	transport transfer translate
un		not	unusual uninhabited
vice		deputy instead of	vice chairman vice captain

SUFFIXES		MEANINGS	EXAMPLES
-able	*-ible*	capable of	suitable edible
-ain	*-an*	connected to	chaplain publican
-ance	*-ence*	in a state of	repentance existence
-ment	*-ness*		amusement hopelessness
-ant	*-er*	someone who	servant grocer
-eer	*-ier*		engineer carrier
-ess		female form	lioness princess
-fy		to make	magnify purify
-less		without	timeless fearless
-ling	*-ock*	little	duckling bullock
-ory		a place for	factory rectory
-ous		full of	monstrous victorious

Punctuation marks

A full stop is used at the end of a sentence.

- It is becoming more common to omit full stops for initials and abbreviations:

    A.A. or *AA*   *B.B.C.* or *BBC*
    department/*dept*   Limited/*Ltd*

, A comma is used to separate phrases in a sentence, or when a list is being written. When reading aloud, pause at a comma.

    John, bring me some groceries please.

A semicolon is a full stop above a comma. It is used to join two sentences instead of a conjunction.

    Mind that paint; it is wet.

A colon is used before a list, or to introduce sayings or ideas.

    Many people came: painters, architects, draughtsmen and engineers.
    The law says: wear a seat belt.

! An exclamation mark is used after interjections which indicate surprise, amazement, shock or delight, or at the end of a sentence.

    Oh! Ah! Goodness! Help!
    What a lovely surprise!

? A question mark is used at the end of a sentence, instead of a full stop, when something is being asked.
> *What are you doing?*

" " Inverted commas are used to indicate speech in a sentence. They surround the exact words which are being spoken.
> *"Do you want to play with my toys?" Deborah asked Graham.*
> (See direct and reported speech section, pp 36-37)

- A hyphen is used to join two or more short words:
> *jack-in-the-box*
or between syllables of one word split between two lines of writing. Try to avoid this wherever possible.

"What are you doing?"

( ) Brackets are used around additional words which are not essential to the main part of the sentence but which supply more information:
> *John Bunyan wrote part of* Pilgrim's Progress *(published 1678) in prison.*

* An asterisk is sometimes used to draw your attention to a note giving more information at the bottom of a page.

Direct speech

" " or ' ' are inverted commas, also known as quotation marks or speech marks.

The actual words spoken are put inside the inverted commas. In the above cartoon, there are several ways to write what's being said:

- *Brian said, "Watch out, James! You are too close to that tree."*
- *"Watch out, James!" Brian said. "You are too close to that tree."*
- *"Watch out, James! You are too close to that tree," said Brian.*

Everything inside the speech bubble goes inside the inverted commas.

Question marks and exclamation marks also go inside the inverted commas, because they are a part of the sentence being quoted.

James asked, "What shall I do now? My line is tight."

When a spoken sentence is broken in two by the verb of saying (*said*, *shouted*, etc), the inverted commas are used like this: *"Watch out, James!" Brian said. "You are too close to that tree!"*

To avoid repetition of the words *said* and *asked*, try to use a variety of similar verbs to indicate speech:

*exclaim   reply   answer   shout   tell   demand
enquire   explain*

Reported speech

No inverted commas are needed for reported speech because the exact words spoken are not used.

Brian told James to watch out. He was too close to the tree. James wanted to know what he should do then. His line was too tight.

Reported speech is used in newspaper articles, TV news broadcasts and when someone is telling another person about an event which has already happened.

Word origins

Many of our words have their origins in the Greek, Latin and French languages. Some have been taken from such sources as Russian, German, Indian and American Indian words. New words are still being made and used, particularly in science and technology, and many of these come from Latin and Greek.

Greek origins

ENGLISH	GREEK	ORIGINAL MEANING	PRESENT DAY MEANINGS
biology	*bios*...	life, living organisms	the study of living things, their structure, etc
	logos...	speech or reason	
technology	*techne*...	art, skill	practical or mechanical sciences
	logos...	speech or reason	
calligraphy	*kallos*...	beauty	beautiful writing, as an art form
	graphia...	writing	
chaos	*khaos*...	time before the universe was ordered	utter confusion and disorder
palindrome	*palin*...	again	a word or phrase which reads the same backwards and forwards – eg *ewe*
	dromos...	course or race	
pseudonym	*pseudo*...	false	a fictitious name
	nym...	name	
telephone	*tele*...	far	an instrument for relaying a voice over long distances
	phone...	sound, voice	

Latin origins

ENGLISH	LATIN	ORIGINAL MEANING	PRESENT DAY MEANINGS
audience	*audire...*	to hear, listen to	a group of listeners or viewers
agenda	*agere...*	to do, act, set in motion	things to be done
capture	*capere...*	to take, seize, take prisoner	to take someone prisoner; seize a place
captain	*caput...*	head	the leader, someone in charge of team, etc
dictionary	*dicere...*	to speak, say, tell	a reference book of words, arranged alphabetically, to give meanings, pronunciations, etc
decimal	*decem...*	ten	number system based on tens
educate	*educare...*	to lead out or draw out	to teach, instruct
fraction	*frangere...*	to break	a part of a whole
interrogate	*rogare...*	to ask	to question closely
lavatory	*lavare...*	to wash	a toilet, WC
sinister	*sinister...*	left (Romans thought the left suspect, not normal)	evil, treacherous
dexterity	*dexter...*	right (normal)	skill in using the hands or body

ENGLISH	LATIN	ORIGINAL MEANING	PRESENT DAY MEANINGS
script	*scribere...*	to write	a written or printed text
nature	*natus...*	to be born	animal and plant life
transport	*trans...* *portare...*	across to carry	to move something from one place to another
translucent	*trans...* *lucere...*	across to shine	allows light to shine through
video	*videre...*	to see	visual record

French origins

ENGLISH	FRENCH	ORIGINAL MEANING	PRESENT DAY MEANINGS
chef	*le chef*	the chief, leader	principal cook in a restaurant
café	*le café*	coffee	a small inexpensive restaurant
journal	*la journée*	day	a daily record book, periodical
in lieu	*le lieu*	place	instead of

Miscellaneous origins

ENGLISH	SOURCE	ORIGINAL MEANING	PRESENT DAY MEANINGS
assassin	Arabic *hashshashin*	one who takes hashish	a murderer, especially political killings
geyser	old Norse *geysa*	to gush	a hot water spring
ghoul	Arabic *ghul*	he seized	an evil spirit, grave robber
bungalow	Hindi *bangla*	house	a one-storey house
gymkhana	Hindi *gendkhana*	ball house	a horse riding event
khaki	Urdu *khak*	dust	dull coloured cloth for army uniforms

Words taken from people's names

pasteurise	*Louis Pasteur 1822-95*	French scientist	to heat milk to destroy the bacteria in it
Fuchsia (say *few-sha*)	*Leonard Fuchs 1501-66*	German botanist	flowering plant
spoonerisms	*W A Spooner 1844-1930*	English clergyman	mixing up initial letters eg *a gritty pearl* for *a pretty girl*
wellingtons	*Duke of Wellington*	wore black leather knee high boots	waterproof boots
cardigan	*Earl of Cardigan*	fought in Crimean War	a knitted button-up jacket

17 Mayfield Avenue
Fairfield Green
Washford
Cumbria
TN0 6AH

Letter writing

Letters should contain certain pieces of information in the correct order:

- the full address of the sender, including the postcode in the UK
- the date written
- the receiver's name
- the information
- the correct ending
- the sender's name

The way you begin and end a letter depends on who is to receive it:

To someone you do not know:
To a business group:
To a group of unknown people:

Dear Sir,
Dear Madam,
Dear Sir or Madam,

and end:

Yours truly, or
Yours faithfully,
plus your signature

To someone whose name you know but is not a close friend:

Dear Mr and Mrs Roe,

and end:

Yours truly, or
Yours sincerely,
plus your signature

Yours faithfully
Leslie Blake

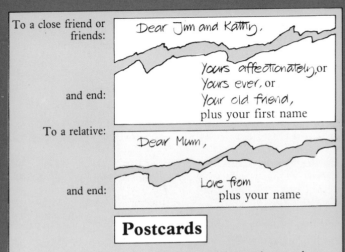

To a close friend or friends:

Dear Jim and Kathy,

and end:

Yours affectionately, or
Yours ever, or
Your old friend,
plus your first name

To a relative:

Dear Mum,

and end:

Love from
plus your name

Postcards

People use postcards for messages which are short and are not private. The sender's address is not needed.

Dear John
  Everything arranged
for weekend.
  Leave Sunday 4 p.m.
Hope to see all the family.

        Love Isabel

John Rushbrook
Moor Cottage
Crossways
BUDE
Cornwall
E2H 466

If a plain postcard is used, put the message on the blank side and the address in the space provided. Make sure to leave room for a stamp!

To Royalty

Letters to Royalty should be addressed to their Private Secretaries.

Start letter	*Address envelope*
Your Royal Highness	His/Her Royal Highness
to Royal Princes/Princesses or Royal Dukes/Duchesses	The Prince/Princess of... or the Duke/Duchess of...

To the Prime Minister

Dear Prime Minister	The Rt. Hon (Name) M.P.

To the Clergy

Church of England

Archbishops:	Dear Archbishop	The Most Rev and Rt Hon the Lord Archbishop of...
Bishops:	Dear Bishop	The Right Reverend the Lord Bishop of...
Vicars & Rectors	Dear Mr	The Reverend John or The Rev John and Mrs if wife included

Roman Catholic Church

The Pope:	Your Holiness Most Holy Father	His Holiness the Pope
Cardinals:	My Lord Cardinal	His Eminence the Cardinal Archbishop of...
	Your Eminence	His Eminence Cardinal if not Archbishop
Archbishops:	Dear Archbishop Your Grace	His Grace the Archbishop of...

Bishops:	My Lord Bishop	The Right Reverend
	Dear Bishop	John... Bishop of ...
Monsignors:	Dear Monsignor	The Reverend Monsignor
Priests:	Dear Father	The Reverend John

Addressing Envelopes

Leave sufficient room at the top right for the stamp. Try to balance the address so that it is not too cramped, nor too spaced out. Punctuation may be omitted and the lines may be staggered or level as in *a* or *b* below.

a
Mr and Mrs P Barman
35 Northfield Ave
Buckfastleigh
Devon
DE9 6AB

b
Mr and Mrs P Barman
35 Northfield Ave
Buckfastleigh
Devon
DE9 6AB

Words and phrases

Synonyms: words with a *similar meaning*.

accuse/blame	rapid/quick	elude/escape
abandon/leave	regret/sorrow	courage/bravery
acute/sharp	coarse/rough	disaster/calamity
stern/strict	dusk/twilight	odour/smell

Antonyms: from the Greek word meaning *opposite name*.
Antonyms are words with *opposite meanings*.

Adjectives
cheap/expensive
difficult/easy
false/true
negative/positive
opaque/transparent
deep/shallow

Nouns
birth/death
war/peace
heads/tails
noise/silence
retreat/advance
famine/abundance

Verbs
to love/to hate
to win/to lose
to shout/to whisper
to find/to lose
to deny/to admit
to buy/to sell

Cheap 20p

Expensive £5

Birth

Love

Hate

Death

DAILY NEWS
BRUTAL MURDER

46

Homophones: from the Greek word meaning *similar sound*. These are words which sound alike but have different meanings.

air/heir
bare/bear
cereal/serial
die/dye
fair/fare
herd/heard
leek/leak
meet/meat
pair/pear
sail/sale
see/sea

throne/thrown
waste/waist

Bare/Bear

Proverbs: a proverb is a short, easily remembered phrase about an everyday fact:

Many hands make light work...
   A job is done more quickly if everyone helps.
The early bird catches the worm...
   Be early if you want something special.
Birds of a feather flock together...
   People with similar interests get on well.
Half a loaf is better than none...
   Be grateful for anything you have.

Similes: a simile compares two similar things using the words *like* or *as*.

as black as coal
as cool as a cucumber
to run like the wind
as quick as lightning
as slippery as an eel
as poor as a churchmouse
as wise as an owl

Metaphors: from the Greek word meaning *to transfer*.

A metaphor compares two things without using the words *like* or *as*:

> *He was a lion in battle.*

(The characteristics of the lion are transferred to the man.)

The metaphor would become a simile if we used *like* or *as*:

> *He was as brave as a lion in battle.*

 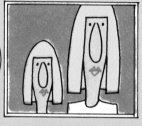 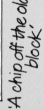

'A chip off the old block'

Colloquialisms: from the Latin word for *conversation*.

A colloquialism is a colourful phrase used in conversation.

> *a chip off the old block*...describes a child who is very like its parent.
>
> *a rough diamond*...is someone who may have rough manners but has good intentions.
>
> *a wet blanket*...is someone who dampens other people's enthusiasm.

Colour associations: Colours are often used in speech to help to describe a meaning:

Red

> *a red herring* is not a fish but a false clue to lead someone off the scent.
>
> *to see red* is to be very angry.
>
> *to be in the red* is to spend more money than you have.
>
> *a red letter day* is a very special day.

Other colours are used too:

> *green-eyed monster*...jealousy
>
> *he's yellow*...he's a coward
>
> *blue blood*...belonging to an aristocratic family
>
> *black sheep of the family*...a disgrace to the family
>
> *a white elephant*...something of little value

Surname origins

The origins of some surnames are obvious eg *Archer*, *Carpenter*. Others are more obscure because they may have changed considerably since they were first used. Surnames or family names are not like first or given names. The surname grew out of the need to distinguish one John from another: *John the cook* or *John the barber*. Where he lived may have been the way to identify him: *John on the hill* or *by the brook*. He may have had a very distinctive appearance such as *John the wild*, *John the longfellow* or *John the whitehead*.

It is thought that by the reign of Richard II (1377-1399) surnames were fixed and no longer referred to the persons bearing them.

Here are some interesting examples:

Occupations
Cooper...*made barrels*
Cutler...*made knives*
Fletcher...*made arrows*
Smith...*made things from metal*
Turner...*made small wooden bowls*

Home or Place of Birth
Fleming *(from Flanders)*
Hawthorne
Sykes *(very small stream)*
Thorp(e) *(small village)*
Greenwood

Appearance or Character
Jolly
Spenlow *(spend love)*
Shakespeare
Armstrong

Others
Elsie...*elf warrior*
Darwin...*dear friend*
Edward...*rich guard*
Godwin...*good friend*

The calendar

DAYS OF THE WEEK:

Sunday means Sun's day. People once worshipped the sun as a god because of its importance to agriculture. The Romans named Sunday.

Monday means Moon's day. The Anglo-Saxons named a day after the moon to please it.

Tuesday Tiw was the Anglo-Saxon god of war.

Wednesday Woden's day. Woden was Tiw's father. The Anglo-Saxons believed that Woden made the world.

Thursday Thor or Thunor was the god of thunder. It was believed that thunder was the sound of Thor's chariot racing across the sky.

Friday Frigg was Woden's wife and the goddess of love and marriage.

Saturday Saturn was the Roman god of farming.

Anglo-Saxon treasures, including a buckle with a representation of their god Woden.

50

MONTHS OF THE YEAR:

January Janus was the Roman god with two faces, one facing forwards, one backwards. He was the doorkeeper of the year.

February *Februare* in Latin means to purify. The Romans had a period of religious purification similar to Lent.

March This was originally the first month of the year, named after Mars, the Roman god of war.

April The meaning is uncertain but it may be from the Latin word *aperio* which means *I open* and may refer to buds and flowers.

May There are two theories: one that May is named after Maia, the Roman goddess, the mother of Mercury; or after Maiores, the senior branch of the Roman government.

June From the Latin Junius, a Roman aristocratic family to which Brutus, one of Julius Caesar's assassins, belonged.

July This month was originally named Quintilis and was the fifth month of the year. It was renamed in honour of Julius Caesar.

August was originally Sextilis (6th month). It was renamed after Augustus Caesar, nephew and heir of Julius.

September was originally the seventh month. *Septem* is Latin for seven.

October was the eighth month before the alteration. *Octem* is Latin for eight.

November was the ninth month…*novem* is Latin for nine.

December was the tenth month…*decem* is Latin for ten.

Hadrian's Wall; frontier of the Roman Empire.

NFWI National Federation of Women's Institutes

NSB National Savings Bank

NSPCC National Society for the Prevention of Cruelty to Children

NT National Trust

NUGMW National Union of General and Municipal Workers

NUM National Union of Mineworkers

NUS National Union of Seamen; Students

NUT National Union of Teachers

OBE Order of the British Empire

OHMS On His/Her Majesty's Service

OPEC Organisation of Petroleum Exporting Countries

OU Open University; Oxford University

PA personal assistant; publicity agent; Press Association

PAYE pay as you earn (income tax)

P&L profit and loss

P&O Peninsular and Orient (shipping line)

PC Police Constable; Parish Council; post card

PDSA People's Dispensary for Sick Animals

PE Physical Education

PhD or **DPhil** Doctor of Philosophy

PLO Palestinian Liberation Organisation

PO Post Office; Petty Officer; Personnel Officer; Pilot Officer

PTA Parent Teacher Association

PTO please turn over

PS Police Sergeant; Private Secretary; post script

QC/KC Queen's/King's Counsel

QED Quod erat demonstrandum (which was to be shown)

RAC Royal Automobile Club

RADA Royal Academy of Dramatic Art

RAF Royal Air Force

RC Roman Catholic

RE Religious Education; Royal Engineers

RUFC Rugby Union football club

RIP rest in peace

RN Royal Navy

RNLI Royal National Lifeboat Institution

ROSPA Royal Society for the Prevention of Accidents

RSPB Royal Society for the Protection of Birds

RSPCA Royal Society for the Prevention of Cruelty to Animals

RSVP Répondez s'il vous plait. (French for please reply to an invitation)

SAYE save-as-you-earn

SLR single lens reflex (camera)

STD subscriber trunk dialling (telephone)

TGWU Transport & General Workers' Union

TNT trinitrotoluene – explosive

TUC Trades Union Congress

UAR United Arab Republic

UDI Unilateral Declaration of Independence (a breakaway from parent state)

UDM Union of Democratic Mineworkers

UDR Ulster Defence Regiment

UFO unidentified flying object

UHF ultra high frequency

UK United Kingdom (England, Scotland, Wales & N. Ireland)

UN United Nations

UNICEF United Nations Children's Fund

UNO United Nations Organisation

USA United States of America

USSR Union of Soviet Socialist Republics

VAT value added tax

VC Victoria Cross